# 10 Lessons from New York City
## Schools

### What Really Works to Improve Education

Eric Nadelstern

TEACHERS COLLEGE PRESS

Teachers College,
Columbia University
New York and London

Published by Teachers College Press, 1234 Amsterdam Avenue, New York, NY 10027

*Library of Congress Cataloging-in-Publication Data*

Nadelstern, Eric.
10 lessons from New York City schools : what really works to improve education / Eric Nadelstern.
   pages cm
Includes bibliographical references and index.
ISBN 978-0-8077-5449-8 (pbk. : alk. paper)
   1. Public schools—New York (State)—New York. 2. School improvement programs—New York (State)—New York. 3. Educational leadership—New York (State)—New York. 4. School improvement Programs—United States. I. Title. II. Title: Ten lessons from New York City schools.
LA339.N5N27  2013
371.2'07—dc23                                 2013007229

ISBN 978-0-8077-5449-8 (paper)

Printed on acid-free paper
Manufactured in the United States of America

20  19  18  17  16  15  14  13        8  7  6  5  4  3  2  1

thinker, and successful implementer. A rare combination that makes this book a must-read for any education leader at any level."

—**Sajan George**, founder & CEO, Matchbook Learning

"In *10 Lessons from New York City Schools*, Eric Nadelstern provides a practical framework for achieving a culture of student-focused performance, offers a systemic approach for creating interdisciplinary teams responsible and accountable for student outcomes, and shares compelling real life examples that inspire school leaders to be **bold** in creating an environment of success for students and teachers alike. Through his experience you come to know that the impossible is indeed possible—children can be first in our school systems."

—**Donna Rey**, Chief Administrative Officer, Local 1199 Health and Hospital Workers Union, and former Deputy Chief Operating Officer for the New York City DOE

"Veteran educator Eric Nadelstern knows New York City's public schools inside and out, spending decades fighting battles large and small, in the classroom and out—all the while making sound decisions grounded in improving teaching and learning and on what is best for children. His hard-earned expertise and advice is well worth listening to."

—**Liz Willen**, editor, *The Hechinger Report*

"Eric is truly the renaissance man of New York City public schools. As a student, parent, teacher, mentor, principal, superintendent, and most recently, chief schools officer for New York City public schools, he changed predestined outcomes for thousands of NYC students through his unrelenting focus on improving the unit of change that matters most: the school. This book is saturated with the wisdom of knowing what works and the inspiration to dare to do it!"

—**Veronica Conforme**, COO, New York City DOE

"Having been a principal of a Title I school in the New York City public school system for 23 years, none have been more productive or rewarding for our school than the years we spent in Eric's Empowerment Zone Initiative. Through his visionary leadership of cutting the red tape that bogged schools down, allowing schools to make meaningful decisions as to what was best for their communities, and holding them personally accountable for these decisions, we were able to make our school one of the best in New York City in all-around academic performance. His ideas and recommendations are certainly a must-read for every educator."

—**Lily Din Woo**, principal, P.S. 130M, New York, New York

To the extraordinary women who have shaped my life, and who are the only people in the world who share my surname:

My wife Paula Nadelstern, the love of my life.
My daughter Ariel Nadelstern, the wonder of my life.
My mother Eva Nadelstern, my first teacher.

# Contents

# Acknowledgments

This book would not have been possible without the many thousands of children I have been privileged to work with for over 4 decades in public education, the parents who entrusted their children to my care, and the extraordinary teachers and principals I have worked with and learned from.

# 10 Lessons from New York City Schools

## What Really Works to Improve Education

# Introduction

In 1955, I began Kindergarten in the New York City public schools 1 year after *Brown v. Topeka Board of Education*, the landmark Supreme Court decision that forever struck down the foolish notion that separate could ever be equal. At that time, the high school graduation rate in New York City was about 50%. When I started teaching in the New York City public schools almost 2 decades later, the graduation rate was still about 50%. In 1985, when I opened International High School at LaGuardia Community College, the graduation rate remained at about 50%. I accepted the position of deputy superintendent for new and small Bronx high schools at the start of the new millennium, and at that time, the graduation rate was still about 50%. At the start of Children First (the Bloomberg/Klein Administration) in 2002, only half the students in our schools graduated,[1] just as they had since the middle of the 20th century.

When Joel Klein became the New York City schools chancellor, I was first named deputy regional superintendent for the East Bronx, supervising 116 elementary, middle, and high schools in the poorest, most educationally deprived congressional district in the country. Soon thereafter, I was invited to the Central Office as senior instructional superintendent, and quickly transitioned to chief academic officer of new schools. Over the next 5 years, the Department of Education (DOE) would close more than 100 large low-performing schools, and open over 500 new ones, including more than 100 new charter schools. We also started our own Leadership Academy to train a new kind of principal for these and other schools, which soon produced 70–80 new principals each year. Before long, these new principals complained to the chancellor that we had trained them to reinvent schools so that more students could be more successful, but then placed these schools within the same district and regional organizations that had always existed. Instead of encouraging them to create better schools and practices, these old line district superintendents, supervisors, and administrators would give every reason in the book why the new schools had to do things the way they had always been done, much like the failed schools the new ones were meant to replace. The stepping up to demand what they needed in order to serve students well by this new generation of principals was an early validation of our training of them. As a result, Chancellor Klein approached me in 2004 to develop a new set of school management strategies that would place the schools at the top of the organization, presume that those closest to the students were in the best position to make the important decisions, and assume that the rest of us worked for principals and schools rather than the other way around. This initiative was called the Autonomy Zone.

Empowering strategies that were spelled out in the Autonomy Zone included:

- Those closest to students and teachers in the classroom are in the best position to make the important decisions for a school.
- Principals, in consultation with teachers, parents, and sometimes the students themselves, are in the best position to make those decisions.
- In return for this decision-making authority and autonomy, principals agree to performance contacting.
- The school district's Central Office needs to remove obstacles for principals and their schools, not create them.

The Autonomy Zone quickly grew from 29 schools at the start, to encompass the entire school system within 5 years. In return for being empowered to make the important decisions that influence teachers and students in the classroom, principals signed performance agreements that allowed us to hold them accountable for student achievement for the first time. We used the following indicators to assess student achievement: attendance, retention, school and exam pass rates, promotion, and graduation. Soon we were replacing as many as 50 principals each year and closing half that number of schools to replace them with new small ones, in a process described later in this book.

As of this writing in 2012, New York City public schools are uniquely structured into 60 non-geographic, self-selected, self-governing networks of 25–30 schools each. Instead of proximity, the new networks are based on common philosophies as determined by principals, allowing them to provide mutual support. More important, for the first time in more than half a century, the graduation rate has increased from 50% to 65%. I retired as the deputy chancellor for school support & instruction in January 2011 after 39 years of service. This book identifies the ten most significant lessons in school and school system improvement that I learned from this ground-breaking work. It serves as both a chronicle of the decade in the history of New York City public schools known as Children First, which existed from 2002–2011, and as a blueprint for educators and others interested in restructuring large urban school districts so that more students are more successful.

> I've always been a teacher. Only my students have changed.

Over the course of a career in public education that has spanned nearly 4 decades, I've been a teacher, staff developer, principal, superintendent, deputy chancellor, and now, college professor. I'm neither a researcher nor an academic. However, I've always been a teacher. Only my students have changed.

## CHAPTER 1

# Invest in Leadership

While extolling the importance of talented leadership at all levels of the system, most school districts have done little to identify, recruit, develop, and support the leaders they claim to desperately need. The hope is that such individuals will spontaneously appear, or otherwise drop from the heavens, ready to take on the formidable challenges of leading, if not transforming, some of the most dysfunctional institutions ever created. That this organizational miracle never actually occurs does not seem to deter those engaged in system management by wishful thinking. Rather than decry the dearth of skillful leaders, superintendents need to proactively do something about it.

The New York City Department of Education (DOE), formerly known as the New York City Board of Education prior to 2003, was no different. It was simply assumed for many decades that the natural laws of organizational evolution and human ambition would conspire to produce the effective principals and assistant principals that our schools required. The best would somehow rise to the top, and universities in the City were trusted to train them successfully. After all, New York City boasts a significant number of nationally renowned institutions of higher education.

The results of such a blind faith approach to leadership development ran the gamut. On the one hand, talented district superintendents, (of which there were few), such as Anthony Alvarado on the East Side of Manhattan in District 2, were constantly on the lookout for accomplished educators who could be great principals. Tony had been an effective District 4 superintendent in New York's East Harlem, and had a brief but memorable 9 months as chancellor. I believe that much of the legendary success of District 2 under Alvarado's supervision can be attributed to this never-ending search for effective leaders. I was called for recommendations, as were many others, resulting in a rare concentration of talent in schools on the East Side of Manhattan.

On the other hand, in my native Bronx, one of the most politically corrupt, economically challenged, educationally deprived political jurisdictions in the country, principalships were for sale at one time in the 1970s for $10,000 in cash. The rest of New York fell in between these extremes with devastating results that froze the high school graduation rate at 50% for more than half a century. All that changed in 2002 with Joel Klein's appointment as schools chancellor.

Klein was not the nation's best teacher, but he was the leading antitrust litigator in the country, having successfully argued the United States' case against Microsoft as an assistant attorney general. Mayor Michael Bloomberg, who had only recently been granted control over the city's schools by the state legislature, appointed Klein as chancellor in the hopes of breaking through the vested adult interest within and outside our public school system in favor of Children First, the novel idea and slogan which characterized the Bloomberg/Klein Administration until Klein's departure in January 2011. From the outset, he innately understood that the principal is in the pivotal leadership role in transforming schools, and consciously set out to develop personal relationships with as many as he could through a systematic series of meetings with all principals, and an open invitation to them to email him any time. Joel's email response time remains legendary, and is timed in mere seconds.

Joel Klein also understood that the universities could no longer be relied on to prepare the kind of innovative transformational leaders our schools required. In fact, it was the universities that had prepared the principals of the past who perpetuated structures and practices that resulted in unacceptably high student failure rates. Instead of continuing to rely on colleges to produce the principals needed, Klein used private funds to open the New York City Leadership Academy, an in-house principal preparation and certification program, which produced 70 new principals each year, about half the number required annually.

Some of the academy's most important features included close screening of applicants on paper and by interview; full funding for the year, including a salary somewhere between that of an assistant principal and principal; and a preparation program focused less on managing schools as they currently exist, and more on transforming schools into the institutions we need to educate all youngsters.

While to date there is scant evidence that principals prepared by the Academy outperform those who take a more traditional route, the initiative served to create a cadre of leaders loyal to the chancellor and his efforts to place children first. It also served as something of a wake-up call for those who directed university principal preparation programs that the future was not what it used to be. The following story demonstrates one of the fundamental problems with such programs.

During my tenure as deputy chancellor for school support & instruction, I was approached for a meeting by the Metropolitan Council of Education Administration Programs, an organization that represents university-based principal preparation programs in the greater New York City area. The programs represented by this organization were disturbed by a memorandum I had sent favoring the appointment of the DOE's Leadership Academy grads over its students. After all, we had invested nearly $200,000 per graduate at our academy, and wanted to recoup that investment in their service as principals of our schools.

I agreed to meet, but then it took the better part of a year for them to find a date that allowed for a quorum. By the time we met, I had forgotten the reason they had requested a meeting in the first place. Consequently, instead of attempting to smooth ruffled feathers, I poured oil on the fire by challenging them to become accountable for the impact of their graduates on raising student achievement in our schools. The basis of my critique of traditional principal preparation programs rested on the absence of impact graduates of such programs had on improved student performance and high school graduation rates during the past 50 years.

Toward that end, I requested lists of graduates from each of the 50 or so institutions in attendance, assured them of student confidentiality, offered to track their grads into principal positions, and then disaggregate the performance of students in their schools to determine the success of the principal preparation they had received. Sad to say, not one college represented that day agreed to participate. The irony is, had they done so we would have needed to find a way to overcome legal and human resource restrictions for sharing student information without their consent. Nevertheless, I remain confident that a way can be found, and that such data would yield significant program improvement strategies.

I noticed one other thing about this group of principal preparation program directors and representatives. They were all White. Given that most students in New York City's public schools are African American and Latino, along with many teachers and principals, the absence of diversity in this group was striking. It's true that in the early 1980s our principals profiled similarly, but that was 30 years ago. Today principals in New York City are much more diverse in terms of race, gender, and sexual orientation than they had been 3 decades earlier. I had the clear but disquieting impression that day that time had passed this group of principal developers by.

Returning to Children First, another important contribution to leadership development was breaking with the notion that before you could be an effective principal, you had to be a successful assistant principal. Many of the candidates inducted into the Leadership Academy came directly from the ranks of our most effective teachers. Principal appointments in many of the new small schools similarly relied on talented teachers who had never served as assistant principals. While this represented a dramatic shift from past practice, it stands to reason that the skills, traits, and attitudes required to be a successful organizational leader are most often different from those required to play a supporting role. We overcame protests from the supervisors' union in the City, representing both principals and assistant principals. People often refer to the Council of Supervisors and Administrators (CSA) as the principals union, but assistant

> Many of the candidates inducted into the Leadership Academy came directly from the ranks of our most effective teachers.

principals outnumber principals 4-to-1. Despite the CSA belief that assistant principals make the best principals, we instituted the practice of looking to our best teachers to prepare them to be principals. That practice has continued.

I'm told by those in charge of the DOE today that efforts are underway to systematically identify and cultivate future leaders. The staff I trained and put into place understand how important this work is to the future of our schools. Principals and network leaders are beginning to understand that preparing those they work with for school leadership is the most important aspect of their jobs. With a pool of 120,000 school professionals, and many beyond our borders who wish to come to New York City, there is no shortage of those who can serve as successful principals if we are astute enough to recruit and develop them.

Despite this awareness, and despite the Leadership Academy, the DOE has yet to develop the capacity to create a robust leadership pipeline. The same is true of most large urban school districts in America. Recognizing this fact, those charged with the responsibility in New York City are reaching out to area universities once again. Ironically, I now direct one of the principal preparation programs I criticized earlier in this chapter. In this capacity, I better understand how the DOE's Central Office plays a major role in creating and perpetuating the crisis of leadership in our schools.

Early on in my current position, I realized that we had no systematic plan to place our graduates as school leaders. Therefore, I approached my former colleagues to propose that they participate in our admissions process by identifying promising principal candidates who lack certification credentials, encourage them to apply, and then help us screen applicants to ensure that they met our college entry requirements and expectations for this principal preparation program. For students who were collaboratively admitted, I proposed that the DOE provide scholarship support to be matched by the college for up to 50% of tuition, and guarantee their placement as school leaders in a New York City public school upon successfully completing all requirements. The DOE readily agreed.

Months passed and I did not hear back from my contacts at the DOE. When I finally reached them to ask how many prospective applicants they had identified, the response was none because our program was too expensive, even at half the $48,000 in annual tuition fees. Not prepared to give up just yet, I let them know that we had independently recruited and admitted 40 students who were working in New York City public schools. My fallback suggestion was for the DOE to review the prior performance of these staff members to determine if they wished to support any of them in the manner we had discussed. Once again, the DOE readily agreed.

Several weeks went by. When I reached out to my contacts at the DOE, they responded that they did not recognize any of the students we admitted who were working in their schools. Of course, I assumed that high level district supervisors would not know these individuals personally, but expected them to reach out to superintendents and network leaders who would consult with the principals of the schools where the candidates worked before recommending them. When I communicated that expectation, they asked me to decide instead. I readily agreed.

I wrote to all 40 students to determine their interest in receiving substantial scholarship support in return for working as supervisors in a New York City public school for 3 consecutive years after program completion. To my surprise, only 18 agreed, with the others citing their desire to remain mobile and find their own position. Each of them received $8,000 in scholarship support from the DOE, matched by the same funds from our program for one-third of tuition remission.

The biggest surprise, however, came later from the DOE. They objected to the requirement that these scholarship students were required to commit to 3 years of service after receiving certification, claiming that the department did not have the capacity to keep track of such service. I convinced them that we could all just pretend to monitor that they would work for 3 years.

This experience has made me understand the problems I had perceived with the absence of accountability on the part of university-based principal preparation programs for how their students perform as principals after graduation were not as one-sided as they seemed when I was deputy chancellor. Nevertheless, even now as director of a university program for principal preparation, I view the erosion of the monopoly that colleges had enjoyed as the sole certifying institutions for teachers and principals as an enormously positive development for schools and school districts. As districts begin to compete in this area, along with Charter Management Organizations (CMO) and others providing school management services that put children first, I have every confidence that the resulting choice and competition will lead to more effective leadership preparation both within and outside university programs, as well as greater accountability for supporting these leaders during their service. The resulting differentiated choices for students pursuing principal preparation are more likely to result in innovations that will lead to improvements in the field.

I also firmly believe that schools attract the quality of leadership they are designed to attract. Often superintendents claim there are few strong, innovative principal candidates available, without realizing that by usurping principals' decision-making authority, they are responsible for schools that both require and attract weak leaders. If we want bold, creative school leaders, then we must empower principals to be so. Once accomplished, we will begin attracting those who are bold and creative.

As you will discover in Chapter 5, the small schools revolution in New York City did in fact attract bold, innovative principals. Marc Sternberg, for example, was one such leader. Having graduated from Princeton University, Sternberg was serving as vice president of Victory Schools, a CMO. He was an alumnus of Teach for America, and

> If we want bold, creative school leaders, then we must empower principals to be so.

was attracted to public schools in New York City because of the sense of possibility that new schools offer. After successfully founding Bronx Lab High School in 2004 at the Evander Childs Campus in the northeast Bronx, he became a White House Fellow assigned to the staff of Secretary of Education Arnie Duncan before returning to the New York City Department of Education as a deputy chancellor. Today, Bronx Lab continues to graduate 70% of its students[1] on a campus that once saw its graduation rate plummet to 30%. On the eve of his 40th birthday, Marc had already accomplished a great deal in a career that will likely see him continue to contribute as the superintendent of a major American city.

When he was first running for mayor of New York City, Michael Bloomberg was asked why he thought his experience in the private sector would be applicable to a leadership role in government. The mayor responded that the chief responsibility of a successful manager in any sector is to recruit the best people he or she can find, develop them, support them, incent them when they do good work, protect them from outside interference, and most important, hold them accountable for the highest standard of performance. I have long thought that if a school district invested in leadership development in this way and did nothing else, it would be far preferable to what many superintendents mistakenly believe their jobs to be.

**Bloomberg's Rules for Successful Management**

- Recruit the best people you can find
- Support them
- Provide incentives for good work
- Protect them from outside interference
- Hold them accountable for the highest standard of performance

## CHAPTER 2

# Devolve Responsibility, Resources, and Authority to Schools

There are two basic strategies employed by school superintendents: top-down command and control management, and decentralized authority and decision making. The overwhelming number practice the former by identifying two or three off-the-shelf curricular programs and instructional approaches, mandating that all teachers in all schools adopt these models, organizing Central Office professional development efforts to train teachers and principals on how to implement, and holding schools accountable for complying with the methods and materials chosen. We saw this at the national level with Reading First, with states compelled to adopt or lose federal funding, with hundreds of millions of dollars spent, and in the end, no measurable improvement in student reading.[1] One problem with this top-down strategy is that it is difficult to achieve buy-in from those charged with implementing it; it largely ignores the reality that when teachers close their classroom doors each morning, they do whatever they feel is necessary; it lets school personnel off the hook for raising student achievement since it was the superintendent's idea, not theirs; and, it rarely achieves more than a short-term bump in 4th-grade reading scores, with no gains evidenced in the 8th grade or at high school graduation. Most often, the superintendent has moved on to a new district before the failure to achieve long-term success becomes evident.

The Chancellor's District in New York City, created by former Schools Chancellor Rudy Crew in the 1990s, was a good example of the failure of this kind of top-down, compliance driven district leadership approach. A number of us, including leading

13

educational reformers such as Deborah Meier from Central Park East Secondary School and the Coalition of Essential Schools, Sy Fliegel from the Center for Educational Innovation, and Beth Lief from the Fund for New York City Public Education (later known as New Visions for Public Schools) had put forth a proposal for a "Learning Zone." The central idea was to free up to 50 new small schools, of about 400 students each, from the oversight of the Central Office. These schools were to provide one another with mutual support and common accountability for higher levels of student achievement. It was an early attempt at creating a dramatically decentralized school district which would be held accountable for student performance, rather than the process for achieving it.

At first, Crew pretended to like the idea. It then became apparent that his notion of a Learning Zone would include only the worst schools which would be micromanaged by a new superintendent. Everything including curricula, instruction, textbooks and equipment purchased, staffing, professional development, budgeting, scheduling, and extended school day would be determined by the superintendent and her staff. The initiative was rebranded as the "Chancellor's District."

The results were initially encouraging as 4th-grade reading scores improved for the first few years. But as time went on, it became apparent that at the secondary school level, there were no significant improvements. In fact, a dozen of the former Chancellor's District schools have since been closed due to persistently poor student performance. Despite the failure of this command and control type of district management, it is still held up as a leading example by the teachers union and others who have a vested interest in perpetuating the status quo. They offer the rationale of paying teachers to teach a longer school day, providing them with the curriculum, and training them on how to use it as the way to raise student performance. But they ignore the reality that this top-down approach yields short-term gains in the early grades at best, and that the absence of teachers' ownership for the achievement of their students that results when you tell them what to do, is a failed strategy in the upper grades and in the long term.

For most of my career in the New York City public schools, top-down management from the Central Office was the norm. Not coincidentally, the graduation rate was frozen at 50% during all but the last few years, when we changed our management approach. Of the 14 chancellors I served under, only two practiced a different approach.

Joseph Fernandez came to the DOE in the early 1990s after a successful superintendency in Miami, Florida. His signature program was called School Based Management/Shared Decision Making (SBM/SDM). This was an early form of decentralizing authority to the school level based on seminal advances made by the small school district of Edmonton in Alberta in Western Canada, which had decentralized purchasing resources to schools that could then buy them back from the Central Office or choose to spend their money elsewhere.[2] Pilgrimages from New York City's Central Office to Edmonton were not uncommon during this and the next two administrations.

Despite strong support for SBM/SDM from the teachers union, the concept of shifting the locus of authority from Central to the schools did not catch on. In that respect, Fernandez was ahead of his time. Ironically, however, he subsequently lost his job after mandating a sex education curriculum that attempted to recognize and accept homosexuality.

The other chancellor who practiced a different and decentralized school management approach was Joel Klein. As assistant attorney general during the Clinton Administration, Klein was in charge of the Antitrust Division at the Justice Department. He believed deeply in choice, competition, and differentiation as a means of spurring innovation and developing successful practices. Those beliefs notwithstanding, as chancellor of the New York City Department of Education at the beginning of this millenium, he found himself leading the most intractable top-down bureaucracy since the fall of the Kremlin.

Klein's plan for dismantling central and field operations so that resources and authority could be devolved to schools was nothing short of brilliant. He went from a structure of 40 district superintendents to ten regional ones, eliminating 75% of those organizations and sending thousands of former district staff members back to schools or into retirement. In the process, he saved $200 million, which was redirected to school budgets. Rather than dismiss the former district superintendents and thereby create a strong politically-connected oppositional group, he allowed them to find other positions with the DOE at their old salary levels.

The new regional superintendents were all former district superintendents or their deputies. Rather than following the lead of the chancellor and continuing to devolve resources and authority to their schools, they jealously guarded their authority and adopted the same top-down management approach they had employed previously in their districts. To minimize their opportunity to do so, the chancellor stripped them of budgetary authority and positioned that responsibility in a different part of the Central Office that managed these funds more prudently.

The next step was to pilot a different management strategy that would decentralize authority to principals and schools. This initiative, which I was asked to lead, became known as the Autonomy Zone. The Zone would shift the locus of control from the Central Office to the schools themselves. The idea was to move from a compliance-focused organization to a performance-driven one. To accomplish this, the relationship between schools and the Central Office would need to change dramatically.

Every Zone principal was required to sign a performance agreement, which permitted us to hold them accountable for higher student performance results—something we had never been able to contractually negotiate. In return, the principals, in consultation with teachers, parents, and sometimes students themselves in the higher grades, made the important decisions about staffing, scheduling, curricula, instruction, and assessment that had typically been determined in the Central Office. In return for this new authority regarding the things that matter most in schools, we were able to hold principals accountable for a number of student outcomes, including attendance, retention, course and exam pass rates, promotion and graduation, and, at the high school level, college acceptance.

Autonomy Zone schools outperformed the system average on each measure delineated above. More important, every Zone school outperformed its own results from the previous year.

Although some of these measures, like course pass rates, were internal to these schools, all Zone schools were also required to administer state tests. The gains on standardized reading and math tests in the early grades, and Regents Examination results that led to increased high school graduation rates, were irrefutable. Within a few short years, this decentralized school management strategy would replace the top-down command and control approach previously employed by district and regional superintendents, as well as former chancellors.

I cannot overstate the impact of the devolution of responsibility and authority to schools on district budgetary savings. As an example, when I was deputy superintendent for Bronx High Schools, the district office's share of each school's budget was $650,000 skimmed off the top as a kind of "management fee." As a result, our district staff for the 20 high schools we supervised numbered 120! In contrast today, the management structure at the DOE for 25–30 schools costs about $85,000 per school. The savings of approximately $565,000 per school are now largely in schools' budgets.

In retrospect, I first became aware of the power of decentralizing authority when I opened New York City's first International High School on the campus of LaGuardia Community College in 1985. We established six teams of four teachers who were responsible and accountable for the success of 75 students. Teams had control over their teacher and student schedules, curriculum, instruction, class assessments, teacher hiring when there was a vacancy, and even participated in evaluating each other. We also devolved funds for supplies and materials so that each team had $20,000 per year to purchase materials, go on trips, hire tutors, or even compensate themselves for working with their students after school, on weekends and holidays, and during the summer vacation.

In return, I held each team accountable for high standards of student performance in the same areas that would later become accountabilities for Autonomy Zone schools: attendance, retention, course/exam test rates, graduation, and college acceptance. Although teams could be disbanded if they did not produce student achievement results, it was never necessary to do so. The results were spectacular, with 90% graduating and going on to college. Early findings in an internal review conducted by the City University of New York (CUNY) into how well our students performed in CUNY colleges showed higher rates of retention, credit accumulation, and grade point averages. This was a remarkable achievement since all of our students were English Language Learners. Today, there are 14 International High Schools in New York City and two in California, and it is still considered by advocates and the field to be at the forefront of approaches to educate immigrant adolescents.

It was at International that I first learned that the more authority you share, the more influential you become. This is so because those you empower are usually more disposed to seek out your views and change their behaviors as a result of your opinions. That's an important lesson that most superintendents have yet to

> The more authority you share, the more influential you become.

learn. When they do, it holds the potential for widespread transformation of our schools, leading to significantly higher levels of student achievement.

## CHAPTER 3

# Make Everyone Directly Responsible and Accountable for Student Performance

For the first 30 years of my nearly 4 decades with the New York City public schools, which lasted from 1972–2011, there was little to no accountability for student outcomes. Chancellors came and went every 2 to 3 years on average, but none lost their jobs because students weren't learning or because the graduation rate seemed stuck at about 50%. Neither were superintendents, principals, or teachers held accountable for student performance. Rather, personnel at all levels of the system were evaluated on the basis of how well they got along with their supervisors, whether they could manage those for whom they were responsible, and whether paperwork was submitted in a timely fashion.

In fact, the prevalent but rarely spoken belief was that poverty is determinant, and that schools could not alter outcomes shaped by socioeconomic status. It was widely accepted by school staff at every level that society would need to eliminate poverty before we could improve our schools. As a consequence, student success was not a value because it was assumed that students who succeeded did so due to family income and support. Schools that succeeded with poor students were viewed with suspicion that they were selecting only academically prepared poor kids, getting more than their fair share of resources, or were downright cheating to achieve such results.

I was a public high school principal in New York City from 1985–2001. At one point during that time, the executive director of High School Division invited me to speak with his high school superintendents about the virtues of small schools. Deborah Meier, a MacArthur Award winner and the principal of Central Park East Secondary School, was also invited to share her small school experiences.

After Meier and I spoke about experiences as small school principals, one of the superintendents pointed a finger at Debbie and said, "The only reason why your school is successful is because you carefully screen and select your students." In Debbie's defense, she enrolled a mix of students that reflected her East Harlem community. Then as that finger arced its way through the air in my direction, I feared the worst. "And you," she said, "The only reason that your school is successful is because you don't follow the rules!" Little did she realize that "breaking the rules" is exactly what is required when following the rules doesn't get the job done. As I looked around the room, I realized that all of the superintendents in attendance had been charismatic leaders of large failed schools. Even though they had not raised student achievement during their tenure as principals, their promotions to superintendents were based on their ability to manage and keep a lid on schools with high rates of failure.

For the first several years of the Klein Administration, which began in 2002, there was little focus on accountability for student learning outcomes. Several chief accountability officers came and went with nothing to show for their time in office. One of those accountability officers is now in his second position as superintendent of a small city school district. Across the country, it is not uncommon for superintendents to move on after a few short years due to dismissal or fear of being discovered as a district leader with no good ideas for lasting improvements in student performance.

Regional superintendents in New York City, who had never really been accountable for student achievement, were asked by Central to set growth targets for reading and math scores. With no basis for doing so, each arbitrarily set the numbers as low as they felt would be respectable and acceptable. There appeared to be no incentives for reaching the targets, nor consequences for not doing so. The problem of manipulating targets in education is as predominant as the conviction that the district leader will move on before the results can be assessed. Unfortunately, both are equally true to the present.

Through the Autonomy Zone initiative, we led with principal and school empowerment, but had no systemic and coherent plan to hold them or ourselves accountable for student performance gains. That began to change with the appointment of Jim Liebman as chief accountability officer. Liebman is a civil rights lawyer and anti-death penalty advocate, and is on the faculty at the Columbia University Law School. However, it was Liebman's role as parent of two children in our schools that motivated him to reach out to Klein with suggestions on how to improve accountability for principals and teachers in a way that would raise student achievement. Klein made him put his money where his mouth was by placing him in charge of developing and implementing a robust school accountability system.

As chief accountability officer, Liebman set out to create value-added assessment tools that would permit the chancellor and his staff to compare student progress that each school makes in relation to other schools with similar student populations (on a year-to-year basis). Toward that end, he developed an annual School Progress Report that placed each school in peer groups of 40 schools that profiled similarly on the basis of students served, considering issues like racial composition, socioeconomic status, special education students, English Language Learners, and standardized test scores in the year prior to admission. Based on progress and mastery comparisons with other schools in the peer group, every school was assigned a letter grade of A, B, C, D, or F.

---

**Sorting Schools to Compare within Similar Groups**

- Racial composition
- Socioeconomic status
- Special education enrollment numbers
- Percentage of English Language Learners
- Previous standardized test scores

In addition to School Progress Report grades, schools were also evaluated by a School Quality Review, which consisted of a 2- to 3-day visit by evaluators who looked at the quality of school leadership, classroom instruction, practices of teachers, and the ability of the staff to use data to inform instruction. Quality Reviews culminated in both a report of findings and an assessment designation of Well Developed, Proficient, or Undeveloped. To initially establish this process, the DOE hired Cambridge Associates, the firm that had pioneered a similar review process in Great Britain.[1]

---

**School Quality Reviews**

- School leadership
- Classroom instruction
- Teacher practices
- Use of data to inform instruction

---

In order to develop the skills and strategies that Quality Reviews assessed, each school was required to establish an Inquiry Team. These teams of teachers and supervisors were expected to identify a group of students who were not achieving as well as they should, research why these students were failing to perform, and identify and implement strategies to improve the target group's performance. As expected from a mandate from the Central Office, some schools created effective Inquiry Teams, some were ineffective, and still others only pretended to be so, only going through the motions as a compliance-driven exercise.

To round out the school evaluations, the DOE also annually surveyed teachers and parents. Together with Progress Reports and Quality Reviews, this became the basis for evaluating schools and principals. The bottom 2–3% of the schools were scheduled for closure each year. An additional 3% of principals were replaced on an annual basis as a consequence of poor performance on these instruments.

High school Progress Reports turned out to be a more accurate reflection of student performance than those for both elementary and middle schools. This was because 85% of the latter were based on annual New York State reading and mathematics examinations in grades 3–8. These tests are valid in that scores are a strong predictor of high school completions. For example, a student who scores at the highest level, Level 4, in the 8th grade has a 90% chance of completing high school, whereas the 8th-grader who scores at Level 2 has a 50% chance of doing so. These tests, however, are notoriously unreliable, capable of wild fluctuations from year to year, particularly when the New York State Education Department recalculates the norms, as it did just a few years ago, causing scores to plummet in urban areas throughout the state. On the other hand, the high school reports represent a better balance of internal school measures such as credit accumulation and graduation results, in addition to external New York State Regents Examination results in English, math, science, global history, and American history.

The historic importance of these results was not whether these assessments represented the best and most accurate way to evaluate schools and their leaders. I'm certain that in the years to come, better and more accurate and sophisticated assessment tools will emerge. However, Liebman's work not only established the baseline, but also served to change the conversation. We no longer debate about whether schools, principals, and teachers should, or even can be evaluated; now, the discussion is on how best to evaluate our schools and those who work in them.

Recently, I had a disconcerting talk with the chief financial officer of a for-profit provider of after-school support services. His contention was that school people don't care about student performance. The basis of that contention was that his company's program measurably and significantly raised student performance in a mid-sized city in Texas, but despite that success, the superintendent had discontinued their services for the following year, citing teacher resistance to implementation. "They just don't care about their kids," the CFO lamented.

It's not that schools and districts don't care about student outcomes, it's that they care about them and many other things without prioritizing student achievement above all else. The most important relationship in education is that between students and teachers in classrooms; everyone else in the district needs to work to support that relationship and be accountable for the success of those students. Unfortunately, that is rarely the case.

When you ask personnel in most district offices which schools they are responsible for, they will invariably respond with, "all of them." When you follow up with exactly what they are accountable for, most often you would be met with silence and blank stares. However, if those who work at Central do not feel responsible for student achievement in at least some of the schools they are responsible for, it is difficult to imagine how they will share that responsibility with principals and teachers.

The raging debate in public education these days is about teacher accountability for student performance. The stumbling block appears to be weighing standardized test results. In New York State, standardized and district-developed exams must account for 40% of the total rating score.[2] The relative percentage selected is arbitrary, of course. The important thing is to make the decision about how the remainder of a teacher's evaluation will be determined, and get on with the business of holding teachers accountable for how well their students do. Other accountability measures that are valuable indicators include supervisor, peer, parent, and even student evaluations in whatever percentages and by whatever rubric the district or school feel is important. Good teachers like other professionals already hold themselves accountable for producing results. It's past time to do the same for all teachers. In fact, everyone who works in the district needs to be directly responsible and accountable for the performance results of at least some of the students.

Joel Klein used to tell a story about NASA during the Kennedy Administration. Apparently President Kennedy visited NASA shortly after establishing the goal of putting an American on the

> Good teachers like other professionals already hold themselves accountable for producing results. It's past time to do the same for all teachers.

moon within a decade. During the visit he ran into a janitor in the men's room, and asked him what he did at NASA. "I'm working to put a man on the moon," the janitor replied.

The equivalent to the moon landing in education is the elimination of the racial and socioeconomic achievement gap resulting in universal high school graduation with postsecondary learning opportunities. We will only achieve that goal when everyone in education is personally responsible and directly accountable for the highest levels of student achievement.

## CHAPTER 4

# Reward Success and Exact Consequences for Failure

It would seem obvious that if we wish to accomplish something as vitally important as ensuring that all of our students make progress toward reaching their full potential, that superintendents and school districts need to get the incentives and consequences right for principals and teachers. However, few things in public education are as they seem or should be. Rewarding success and exacting consequences for failure is no exception.

As in most other areas of public service, school employees are not compensated on the basis of talent, commitment, hard work, or even achievement. Instead, salaries are based on longevity in position and college credits earned, even if these credits have nothing to do with the job. I remember applying credit for a graduate course in pottery toward a salary differential as a teacher of English as a Second Language. I can still throw 500 sake cups an hour from a pottery wheel, but have never had occasion to apply that talent in my work as an educator.

When everyone gets paid the same salaries, regardless of time and effort expended or student outcomes, only the most disciplined and self-motivated individuals maintain the quality and intensity of work year after year after year. Many cut back, if not withdraw altogether, simply going through the motions each day with no personal investment. While some remain self-motivated as a matter of personal integrity, you can't rely on that to create effective organizations.

As recently as 2006–2007, only 1% of teachers up for tenure in New York City were denied each year. Surviving 3 years in the classroom nearly always resulted in a lifetime guarantee of employment. Many of the individuals attracted to such a proposition had no business teaching.

In my last years at the DOE, I helped turn things around by suggesting that rather than a rite of passage, tenure was the highest honor that the DOE could bestow on a teacher. As such, it would likely take more than 3 years to achieve, and a decision to defer tenure should be viewed as an opportunity for more time with which to achieve this distinction. The result was that by 2010–2011, three times as many teachers were denied tenure, and 39% had their tenure decision extended.[1]

Despite this change of perception, poor teachers are rarely dismissed. This is true even in the face of evidence that for students 2 consecutive years with poor teachers is nearly impossible to overcome. Our schools will not succeed with all children until we find ways to reward great teachers and get rid of terrible ones.

If teachers are rarely dismissed, the same is true historically for principals. Schools in New York City, like many other urban districts around the country, would fail wave after wave of students, but principals retained their positions unless they were found guilty of theft or gross mismanagement, not held accountable for the failure of their students. Here too, we were able to make inroads during the Klein Administration when in the final years, we were effectively discharging approximately 50 principals a year, or 3%, for persistent educational failure. During my time as deputy chancellor, only one principal challenged the decision to let him go, and he lost the case.

But it is not only problematic that we rarely dismiss incompetent teachers and principals. Equally pernicious is the fact that we don't reward the successful ones. The DOE's bonuses for supervisors are based on narrowly defined contractual criteria that often bear no connection to the extent of student achievement in a school. Teachers' bonuses were negotiated as whole school incentives and made even less sense than the ones for supervisors. Some principals do in fact reward good teachers with opportunities to earn additional income by taking on new responsibilities, but this has never been systemic or coherent. Promotions from teacher to assistant principal, then to principal, and finally, to superintendent, could be viewed as a way to

acknowledge exemplary work, but here too, the process is neither defined and coherent, nor based on past success with raising
student achievement.

Student incentives have never been thoroughly investigated
either. Roland Fryer, an economist from Harvard University,
conducted a study a few years back in which New York City
students received financial rewards when they tested well, but it
was a small, narrowly conceived pilot that did not yield positive
results.[2] Many objected to the idea on the grounds that it under-
mined learning for learning's sake, and backed up their views
with research that extrinsic rewards can be demotivating. Yet
many of those who objected regularly bribe their own kids to
study harder and get good grades. From my perspective, the jury
is still out.

Perhaps the best example of misguided incentives comes in
the form of school improvement grants. Traditionally, the response to low-performing schools was to throw more money at
them. The worst-performing schools were often given millions
of dollars to turn themselves around. These funds were used for
things like hiring more teachers, providing more teacher training, buying more supplies and materials, developing academic
intervention services for students, extending the school day, and
many other strategies that are generally effective in functional
schools. The problem, of course, is that the very people responsible for the failure are least well-positioned to redefine the rules,
roles, and relationships at the school that led to failure in the
first place. Yet year after year, the same schools were awarded
large grants to do just that, in spite of evidence to the contrary
that the infusion of additional financial resources would make
a difference.

Similarly, Title I schools that received Federal grants due
to large numbers of low-performing students would risk losing
those monies as soon as the students performed better. The same
is true of English Language Learners when they learn English
and special needs students once they're mainstreamed. Once
again, the incentives and consequences serve to discourage success and reward failure.

Rather than throwing good money after bad by pouring resources into low-performing schools, it is far better to close

them and give others a chance to do better. Failed organizations never reinvent themselves. In New York City over the last decade, the DOE closed 140 low-performing schools, predominantly large failed high schools.[3] As we will see in the next chapter, the buildings themselves were used to house campus communities of new, small, and most often, more successful schools.

One such low-performing school had 4,000 students enrolled, with 900 freshmen holdovers from the year before it was shut. Barely 30% of its students graduated. This school was known to be a bad place for students when I was in high school, longer ago than I care to remember. I once ran into a retail salesman on a trip to Las Vegas who was older than I, and who graduated from this high school. He said it was a "tough place" for students even in the 1940s!

Another closed high school had only 20% of its students make it to junior year. When I met with the principal and his staff, and presented them with the data, they appeared unphased by the information. Their response was that this is how it had always been as far back as anyone could remember. They went on to say that if we wanted to see improvements, we should give them a better building; provide more resources, including better-prepared teachers; pay them more; and send them better-prepared students. Yes, if we sent them better students we would really see how good they actually are.

At a third large failed high school, there were 1,700 students enrolled, 1,200 of whom were freshmen. Year after year, this school would receive hundreds of incoming students, but students rarely got beyond 9th grade. There were more

> If you would not consider sending your child to such schools, whose children should be sent?

students aimlessly milling about the halls during instructional periods than in classes, and no one seemingly was attempting to do anything about it.

If you would not consider sending your child to such schools, whose children should be sent to those schools? Those who say fix these schools and don't close them, haven't a clue how to do that. In truth, the best strategy we have for failed schools is to close them and give others a chance to do better.

The most cynical act I have ever witnessed in all of my years in public education took place during the Levy Administration at the turn of the millennium. Chancellor Levy had identified the five worst performing elementary schools in the City, and proposed contracting with Edison Schools, a for-profit school management organization, to manage these schools back to health. The teachers union adamantly opposed the idea and worked with community organizers from the Association of Community Organization for Reform Now (ACORN) to rally parents and defeat the proposal. The day after it was decided not to work with Edison, everyone walked away from these schools, and parents had to continue sending their children to one of the five worst elementary schools in the City.

Our schools will not improve until we attract the best teachers we can find, and reward them when they significantly improve student achievement. Similarly, the consequence for persistent low levels of student performance must be to dismiss those teachers and principals who cannot get the job done. When the school is so far gone that nothing else will help, closing it is a more practical choice than keeping it open. Getting the incentives and consequences right is a prerequisite to creating a system of schools in which all children reach the highest levels.

## CHAPTER 5

# Create Small Schools

T he creation of a critical mass of new small schools was the single most important breakthrough strategy of the Klein Administration. Students in the poorest parts of New York City had significantly more and better choices of schools to attend. In my native Bronx, for example, we went from having 22 high schools (including two in New York State receivership), from which youngsters and their families could choose, to over 80 such opportunities in the span of 6 or 7 years. One of Klein's mantras was that he wasn't creating a great school system, but rather, a system of great schools.

New York City has had a relatively long history with new small schools, beginning in the late 1960s with storefront alternative schools. By the early 1980s, these pioneering efforts had been organized under their own alternative high school superintendency, which served to protect and support these new schools, but also to isolate and marginalize them. For the remainder of the decade and into the first few years of the next, new alternative high schools were established one at a time. With the infusion of grant money from the Annenberg Foundation in the mid-1990s, another 60 new small schools were added.

I was fortunate enough to be the founding principal of The International High School at LaGuardia Community College, which opened in 1985. The school serves only recently arrived English Language Learners, and integrates language instruction with content area study so that students acquire the linguistic, cognitive, and academic skills necessary for high school graduation and college and beyond. Ninety percent of our students graduated, and 90% of those went on to college. During the Annenberg years, we began replicating the school so that today, there are 14 in New York City and two in California, as mentioned in Chapter 2. Also during those years, the DOE arranged for me to be on loan to New Visions for Public Schools, a not-for-profit school reform organization, as their first principal-in-residence to help jump-start dozens of new small schools.

During the first years of the new millennium, an infusion of resources from the Bill & Melinda Gates Foundation, Carnegie Corporation, and George Soros's Open Society Institute—made available through New Visions for Public Schools—led to the New Century High Schools initiative. Starting first in the Bronx, and extending next to Brooklyn, large low-performing high schools were phased out and replaced by campus communities of new small schools that shared the same large school buildings. Some buildings housed as many as seven new small schools. Each new small school had a different theme or focus. Students elected to enroll after attending an orientation session and indicating interest in the school on a citywide high school application. The student body of these new schools reflected the racial, economic, and academic composition of the City, and often, the district in which it was situated.

By that time, I had been appointed deputy superintendent for new and small Bronx High Schools. We closed six large low-performing high schools and replaced them with dozens of new schools that shared the same large-school buildings vacated by the old ones. The schools that closed weren't shut down immediately, but did not accept new incoming students and were gradually phased out over 3 to 4 years. This allowed us to grow and nurture the new small schools slowly and carefully, one grade at a time.

Under Klein, the chancellor's office assumed responsibility by creating an Office of New Schools and making small schools a citywide initiative. Placing the initiative directly under the chancellor served both to protect these fledging schools and also to communicate their

> The schools that closed weren't shut down immediately, but did not accept new incoming students and were gradually phased out over 3 to 4 years. This allowed us to grow and nurture the new small schools slowly and carefully, one grade at a time.

importance to the rest of the organization. To the extent that superintendents don't personally own similar new strategic initiatives, the Central Office usually conspires to destroy such efforts.

I had assumed the position of chief academic officer for new schools in 2003. Essentially, we took the process developed for Bronx New Century High Schools, whereby we worked with voluntary school planning teams comprised of educators from our schools, parents, students, and community organization members to support the development of new school ideas. The best of the emerging proposals from this group developed actual schools. In this way, we were able to open more than 30 new small schools each year.

Between 2003 and 2009, more than 100 large failed schools, most of them high schools, were closed.[1] They were replaced with more than 500 new small schools, including 100 charter schools.[2] Buildings that had graduated as little as 30% of their students were now seeing graduation rates, in the best cases, of more than 70%. That this occurred during a time when the New York State Department of Education was raising the passing score requirement for the Regents Exams in five subject areas for graduation, represents a tremendous increase in a relatively brief period of time. As such, replacing large failed schools with new small ones was a breakthrough reform.

Many still confuse the need for small schools with small-sized classes. Small schools are more effective because they are personalized. Every student is well known to at least some of the faculty. When large school dropouts are interviewed, the chief reason given for leaving school was that no one knew who the student was, and didn't even notice that he was gone.

Another important aspect of small schools is that the number of teachers represents the principal's class size. If we're serious about principals being the instructional leaders of their schools, then the number of teachers on staff should represent no more than 20 or so to achieve optimal class size. Twenty students in each class by 20 teachers in a school

> When large school dropouts are interviewed, the chief reason given for leaving school was that no one knew who the student was, and didn't even notice that he was gone.

would suggest an enrollment of about 400 students. In New York City, after much negotiation, we arrived at a school size of 432.

Small may be prerequisite to creating the kind of schools where more students can be more successful, but it's insufficient. A few years ago, former Colorado Governor Roy Rohmer served as superintendent of schools for Los Angeles. He invited me and Robert Hughes, Executive Director of New Visions, to spend a couple of days with him and his deputies to discuss small schools. Los Angeles was about to open a school building to serve 2,400 students, and Rohmer was enlightened enough to want to open four schools of 600 instead.

Hughes and I spent the first day unsuccessfully trying to convince Rohmer and his deputies to open six schools of 400, but they did not buy in to the school size argument put forth above. We then tried to convince them that they should not open these schools fully enrolled from year 1, but rather, slowly phase them in one grade at a time to carefully nurture them. Once again, we were unsuccessful. As I left for home, I couldn't help but remember that small schools structured and functioning like large schools were not likely to be any more successful. In fact, that turned out to be the case in Los Angeles. Michelle Fine, at the City University of New York (CUNY) Graduate Center, refers to such schools as large schools in drag.

Over the course of my work with new small schools, a labor of love over 25 years, I learned five important things:

1.  Large failed organizations, including schools, never reinvent themselves.
2.  Small schools are the most important strategy for promoting educational reform.
3.  Teaming proved to be key to the success of these schools. That is, making a small team of teachers responsible and accountable for a manageable number of students served to overcome faculty isolation, and facilitate identification and generalization of successful practices that raised student performance.
4.  The way adults learn in a school needs to parallel the way you want to see them work with students in

their classrooms. If professional development is leader directed, then expect to see teachers at the front of the room lecturing to students. If you would rather see small-group collaborative learning in classrooms, then work with the faculty in the same way.

5.  You can't reform schools unless you also reform the district's Central Office. (This will be further discussed in Chapter 9.)

Small schools represent the breakthrough strategy in New York City, although this was not the case in numerous other parts of the country. In retrospect, I believe there are three reasons that account for our success with this reform. The first is that the initiative was placed under the watchful eye of the chancellor. When that's not the case, the system will invariably conspire to place roadblocks in the way, if not openly oppose this work. Placing new small schools under the supervision of those who require them to emulate the structures and practices of large failed schools is one way to preclude the possibility of success.

The second reason for why small schools worked so well in New York City was the decision to carefully phase them in one grade at a time. This created the opportunity for strong cultures to take root and grow, and for the leadership to fully develop. Most small school principals have never been principals before, and many of the teachers are new to teaching as well.

The third reason was more controversial. We did not require new small schools to admit special education students or English Language Learners (ELLs) for the first 2 years. Although schools could choose to serve these youngsters, our reasoning was that a new principal and six or seven teachers, many new to the profession, should not be expected to

> The second reason for why small schools worked so well in New York City was the decision to carefully phase them in one grade at a time.

address the most complex issues facing our schools during their first 2 years. Also, new small schools don't have a sufficient resource base in their first 2 years to offer programs and services to the full range of youngsters in the community. By year 3, all of our new small schools were required to admit special needs and ELL students into their incoming classes.

There were advocates who objected to this provision, claiming that ELL and special needs students were not provided equal educational opportunity under the law. The United States Justice Department investigated, but did not find cause for concern because by that time, most of our schools were at least 3 years old and accepting all comers. It is interesting to note that during this period, the high school graduation rate for ELL students went from 35% to 29% briefly, before rising to 45% where it stands today.[3]

Needless to say, this became a controversial decision. However, I still believe that sheltering these fledgling schools during their initial growth and development was key to their success.

# Reduce Teacher Load

S econdary schools in America are based on a factory model that was old when Henry Ford was young. The assembly line in these schools is the daily schedule. Students move along the schedule with bells going off every 40–50 minutes, engaging in a kind of musical chairs exercise; and when the bell rings again, everyone files into new classrooms. Teachers tinker with students for the better part of the next hour, which does not connect to the hour before or after, and then the bells go off again. This dance is repeated seven or eight times each day. The hope is that the whole is greater than the sum of its parts, but it never is. If a student crashes and burns, it becomes difficult to impossible to place responsibility or accountability.

Our elementary schools are a variation of the one room schoolhouse on the prairie strung out as far as the eye can see. Despite our best efforts to the contrary, classes are invariably heterogeneous on the basis of students' prior knowledge, interests, and aptitudes. Teachers work in isolation within their classrooms, rarely working with their peers, and never seeing other teachers teach.

While teacher load is primarily seen as a secondary school issue in terms of total number of students seen each day, it has implications for elementary schools as well. It refers to the number of students that a teacher is responsible for each day, and can have a very significant impact on what teachers are able to accomplish. It is often overlooked as well, obscured by concerns about school and class size.

Take, for example, a high school teacher in New York City who teaches five 42-minute classes each day, a typical workload in a large high school. If each class has 34 students enrolled, which is both the contractual maximum and the norm, that teacher has a total student load of 170 youngsters. It's difficult to remember the names of 170 students, let alone get to know each well enough to personalize education.

My daughter Ariel attended a large, well-known high school for the arts in Manhattan. During my first open school visit in the fall of her freshman year, I noticed that her teachers had no idea who she was and could only speak about her from minor notations made on a small card known as a Delaney Card. Placed in a slot of a Delaney Book designed for such purposes, the Delaney Card revealed which class she was in, and what her seat in that class was. These teachers had a daily student load of approximately 170 students.

I quickly surmised that the most I could do for Ariel during such a visit was to get her teachers to take notice of her. Beginning with the 10-minute conference with her English teacher, I interrupted a generic diatribe about class expectations and told the teacher that I did not know what he was doing in class, but whatever it was, my daughter had been completely transformed. She no longer spent hours watching TV or playing video games, but instead, was now so engrossed by Dickens that she could not put down the copy of *Great Expectations* that the teacher had given her. The English teacher smiled, looked over at Ariel as if he was seeing her for the first time, and gave her a hug.

Seeing how well this strategy worked, I now tried it teacher after teacher. My daughter developed a newfound interest in science, and couldn't get enough of the Discovery Channel and *Nova*. Next, "I couldn't get her to stop doing math problems and notice the mathematical underpinnings of everyday activities." Then, her recent fascination with history had caused her to abandon sitcoms in favor of CNN and the History Channel. They had all transformed her life, and in each case, the teacher's response revealed an interest in my daughter that was not evident during the first minutes of the conference. On the way home that evening, Ariel turned to me to say that she had no idea she was doing so well in school!

Al Shanker, the legendary teacher unionist, was made even more so by Woody Allen in his movie *Sleeper* (1973). The plot has Allen waking up after centuries only to discover that the end of civilization as he knew it could be explained by "some guy named Shanker got his hands on an A-bomb in the 20th century." Like many thousands of teachers of my generation, I knew Shanker simply as Al.

Perhaps the greatest impact Al Shanker had on me as an impressionable young teacher was in an article that he wrote for *American Teacher*, published by the American Federation of Teachers during his tenure as its president. In it he describes a hypothetical middle school English teacher who has five classes of 30 students for a student load of 150. Shanker went on to explain that if this teacher assigned two brief 150 work compositions each week, and it took an average of 7 minutes to grade each, then it would take 159 full school days just to grade those papers. Al understood the importance and implications of teacher load.

I was in Brazil several years ago, in the city and province of Sao Paolo, recruited by the Braudel Foundation to evaluate the schools for the State Ministry of Education. After several school visits, I noticed that there was no student work in evidence. When I asked principals and teachers about this fact, they didn't know what I was talking about at first. Then they would mutter something about how the work was taken down because the school had recently been painted.

It was in speaking with several high school teachers in their faculty room that I discovered the answer to this mystery. Each of them taught five classes of 40 students every day for a teacher load of 200! To make matters worse, school only lasts for 4 hours a day, and to make ends meet, these teachers would work in two or three schools. Their student load was 400–600! No wonder they never assigned written work for their students to hand in.

I was first made aware of the question of teacher load by Ted Sizer, the founder of the Coalition of Essential Schools and former dean of the school of education at Brown University. Sizer argued that student load could be reduced significantly without adding costs to the school budget. At first, I was incredulous, but soon I came to understand that simply by creating more double period classes, the number of students that each teacher was responsible for could be reduced by as much as 40%. To illustrate, the same hypothetical middle school teacher referenced earlier in this chapter had five classes of 30 students for a total load of

150 students. However, if two of these classes were double periods, this teacher's load would be reduced to 90 students, or 40% fewer than 150.

Some small schools took the teacher load issue further. At Central Park East Secondary School (CPESS), teachers taught two classes; one in the morning, and a second in the afternoon. Students had one teacher for Humanities (English and social studies), and another for math, science, technology (MST), which also allowed teachers to integrate their subject matter. If average class size was 30 students, then total student load would be 60 students. However, schools like CPESS reduced class size to between 20 and 25 students by cutting down on the number of administrative, clerical, and support positions. Total student load for teachers at that school was 40 to 50 students.

At my own International High School at LaGuardia Community College, average class size was 24 students. Teachers taught three 70-minute periods each day. Six interdisciplinary teams of four teachers were each responsible and accountable for 72 students for 2 years. This major structural shift from the more traditional high school schedule made possible significant student achievement gains. Needless to say, I became a big believer in reducing teacher load as a school reform strategy to raise student performance. And I'm not the only one.

William Ouchi is a professor of business at UCLA. He has studied decentralized decision making in school districts across North America, and was an important influence for both Joel Klein and myself. Ouchi understood that when principals are granted autonomy, they use their resources more wisely than when the Central Office makes those decisions for them. His landmark research findings on decentralization in nine major urban school districts in the United States was entitled *The Secret of TSL*[1] (Total Student Load), after discovering that principals tend to use their newfound budgetary empowerment to hire more teachers and fewer out-of-classroom personnel, thus reducing teacher load.

Earlier in this chapter I mentioned that teacher load was not exclusively a secondary school issue. In elementary schools, the student load issue should not be confused with class size, although in the literal sense, they are one and the same. The distinguishing teacher load issue in the early grades is the ease and frequency with which teachers can provide one-on-one and intensive small group instruction. Generally isolated from other teachers within their classrooms, such opportunities to individualize are few and far between.

I've noticed in urban elementary schools with high concentrations of youngsters living in poverty, which makes the schools eligible for Federal Title I supplementary funding, that there can be as much as one-third of the teaching staff who don't have full-time classroom responsibilities. These teachers are cluster relief teachers, instructional coaches, specialty teachers such as art and music, computer coordinators, and often, the schools' librarians. What if every teacher in these schools had full-time classroom teaching responsibilities? In that case, it would be possible for three teachers to share two classes of 50–60 youngsters in total. The classes could be on the same grade level, or on two contiguous grades so that the teaching team could loop with their students for 2 years. Each team would be responsible for integrating the arts, physical education, and technology; with specialists on a given team serving as a resource for other teachers, but not teaching all students.

Teachers on a team could spell each other for breaks, preps, and lunch periods. More important, the school could ensure that at least one teacher on every team was a master teacher. This structure in and of itself represents the most effective form of professional development. What better way than team teaching for teachers to learn from one another, and identify and generalize successful practice?

Most important, this teaming approach in elementary schools would provide ample opportunity for individual and small-group instruction and tutorials. Yet despite the obvious benefits, I have yet to convince a principal that this would represent a better elementary school experience for children and their teachers. They argue that specialty teachers are instrumental, and that despite the fact that elementary school teachers are generalists entrusted to teach literacy, mathematics, science, and social studies, they're not able to integrate the arts or provide sufficient physical activity for their youngsters. Sometimes, it's simply not enough to have a great idea, but all great schools are built from good ideas.

## CHAPTER 7

# Focus Relentlessly on Improving Student Learning

Schools perform many functions. They provide child care while parents are working, feed children two meals each day, attend to immunization requirements and other health care needs, provide counseling to students and their families, connect youngsters and their guardians to social service providers, and of course, attend to students' learning needs. Schools exist in every community, and often serve at the center of a network of services for children and their families. Despite this broad mandate, none of the services that schools provide are as important as the core mission of teaching and learning. In too many cases, the school's instructional program is the only hope youngsters have to become full participants in the political and economic life of society.

Similarly, principals can easily be distracted from their primarily responsibility as instructional leaders by their many roles and functions. Too many principals hole up in their offices and lose themselves in the myriad required reports, surveys, tasks, and assignments that often distract them from their instructional responsibilities. I've been in schools where the students can't even identify their principal.

The principal is the school's principal teacher. The principal's class is her teachers. The way a principal works with her teachers often determines the way teachers work with students.

As a superintendent, and later as Deputy Chancellor for School Support and Instruction for the New York City Department of Education, I have conducted thousands of school visits. My goal for each visit was to ascertain and further develop the principal's capacity for instructional leadership, help the principal develop a framework for identifying where teachers were on a developmental continuum, suggest strategies for differentiated professional development (PD), and motivate that principal to want me to return in the future because she valued my input. However, with responsibility for 1,700 schools in my last position as deputy chancellor, I was rarely able to return to a school.

---

**Goals When Visiting Schools
as Supervisor of Instruction:**

- Ascertain and further develop the principal's capacity for instructional leadership,
- Help the principal develop a framework for identifying where teachers were on a developmental continuum,
- Suggest strategies for differentiated professional development (PD), and
- Motivate that principal to want me to come back in the future because she valued my input.

---

The visit was usually scheduled for 90 minutes. For the first half hour, the principal would acquaint me with the school, and I would elicit a framework for understanding teacher development in the principal's own words. Frequently, it would look something like this:

**Stage 1:** Classroom Management/Student Engagement
**Stage 2:** Student Product
**Stage 3:** Student Assessment
**Stage 4:** Mentoring Colleagues

In other words, can the teacher regularly engage her students; once engaged, are the students producing a wide range of different work products reflective of their learning; and, how is the teacher evaluating these products to determine what it is that each student needs to do next to move closer to his full potential? If a teacher mastered the first three stages, then she should be used to mentor other colleagues. I would then ask the principal to estimate the percentage of teachers in the school at each of these stages of development. Most classrooms I visit are led by Stage 2 teachers.

The next 40 minutes were spent visiting classes. We would conduct 3–5 minute classroom walkthroughs, and after each, I would ask the principal to determine which stage of development that teacher was on before asking what the principal was working on with that teacher. Rarely did I get a coherent response. Rather, the principal would often attempt to psychoanalyze the teacher.

For the final 20 minutes, we would return to the principal's office. The discussion would involve how to use the framework to get the school's leadership team on the same page, develop strategies for working with each of the levels to move teachers to the next level, and assign responsibilities for each level of professional development to the school's supervisory staff. Supervisors, including the principal, would each be responsible for fostering the development of teachers at a single level. Most often, schools make these assignments by grade level or subject area, but teachers' developmental needs cut across those designations. I would always conclude with the things that impressed me about the school. These were harder to identify in some places than others, but I always managed to highlight at least a few strengths.

> If we want teachers to assess students' needs to drive instruction, rather than simply follow the sequence of topics in textbooks, then principals need to do the same for their teachers.

The point of this exercise is that if we want teachers to assess students' needs to drive instruction, rather than simply follow the sequence of topics in textbooks, then principals need to do the same for their teachers. They must engage their teachers, (understanding that every meeting agenda is an excuse for a lesson plan), organize PD so that teachers produce a wide array of different work products, assess those products to determine what each teacher needs to learn and do to move to the next stage, and co-opt the best teachers to support their colleagues.

By modeling this process for teachers, teachers will be better positioned to do the same with their students.

Early in my career, I took a hard line against standardized assessments. I understood how these examinations reinforced teacher-directed test preparation sessions instead of authentic learning resulting in projects and products of learning. As a superintendent, I came to understand that some form of standardized testing is required to compare the performance of schools in a systematic way. However, evidence of learning must extend beyond test scores.

In too many schools today, there is little to no student work in evidence. On the elementary school level, there is ample evidence of teacher work in each classroom, but rarely more than a two- or three-paragraph student composition, or several solutions to math problems, posted on the walls. This modest work is nearly always two-dimensional and insubstantial. It often represents one night's homework, or the work of a single class period, or the results of a class test. As a consequence, many teachers don't know what good work looks like. Too many principals don't either.

> Evidence of learning must extend beyond test scores.

The only question I used to ask principals that would elicit stranger responses than, "What are you working on with that teacher?" was "What's the best piece of student work you've seen all year?" While some could speak about great teacher work in the form of a unit, lesson, or assignment they were aware of, very few principals could actually speak with authority about a great piece of work that one of their students completed.

I still remember the best student projects I have ever seen, even though I haven't been a high school principal in more than a dozen years, and some of this work took place 15 or more years ago. During a math lesson in which the teacher had given the class three geometric shapes (circle, triangle, and rectangle) with the same area, students were asked to come up with a way to determine which shape was most efficient. One group brought in all the pennies they could find, and proceeded to find out which shape could contain the most pennies. They determined it was the triangle, but that's not what impressed me.

One student observed that each concentric circle of pennies had exactly six more pennies than the previous one. The group set out to discover what this meant. They collected quarters from those present in class, including me, and carefully recorded to whom these needed to be returned. Once again, each successive concentric circle had exactly six more quarters than the previous one.

Now the students were really excited. They went down to the cafeteria and returned with 6-inch paper plates. Yet again, each successive concentric circle of paper plates had exactly six more plates. They asked the math teacher what this meant. He confessed he didn't know, but sent them down the hall to the physics teachers who indicated that they had discovered Pi, or 3.14 (actually 3.14159265359), and that each successive circle had 2 Pi more than the previous, or 6.28, which looked like 6. Having discovered Pi (a mathematical constant that is the ratio of a circle's circumference to its diameter), these students were certain to never forget it from that day forward. I know that I haven't.

I also remember a science project in which a student was attempting to ascertain the differences in sight characteristics between carnivores and herbivores. She talked her way behind the exhibits at the Museum of Natural History in New York City, and over time was able to make plaster of paris molds of the skull of an elk and a cheetah. She then shone a light through the eye sockets of each in a dark room and measured the arc and direction of light that shone through each mold to determine that carnivores have better direct or frontal vision with which to hunt down elk and other prey; and herbivores have better peripheral vision to avoid cheetahs and other carnivores.

These were impressive discoveries representing outstanding student work. There are lessons these teachers can teach us all:

1. The lessons were open-ended,
2. Students were encouraged to take the projects as far as they could,

3.  Other institutions served as resources,
4.  Teachers were not afraid to admit that they didn't know
    something and to direct their students to colleagues, and
5.  Students were encouraged to rely on themselves and
    each other to support their own learning.

The best teacher work I've ever seen was a bridge project for
which a science teacher joined forces with a math colleague. Students were once again in small collaborative groups to research
and build a replica of an existing suspension bridge. Each student
in the group was required to participate in the bridge's construc-
tion and be able to speak compellingly of the math required, as
well as the actual bridge's history. While in most classes, some
students do great work, others do mediocre work, and still others do unacceptable work, every student in this heterogeneous
class of English Language Learners participated in the building
of an outstanding bridge replica, and each could speak power-
fully about the math and history behind it. This was the only
example I have ever seen of an unscreened class in which all
students excelled.

Every teacher in a school needs to know what good work is,
and have concrete images of it. To accomplish this, the principal and school community need to focus on getting kids to
produce as much as possible as a reflection of what they've
learned. By year's end, student work should be spilling out of
classrooms, with teachers collaboratively examining the work
to determine how good is good enough and how to make it better. In schools where this is the case, you can safely assume
that the staff is focusing relentlessly on improving student performance. Nothing less will ensure that all students achieve at
the highest levels.

## CHAPTER 8

# Partner with the Private Sector

The 20th century has been referred to as the American Century. For most of it, the United States garnered the lion's share of the world's resources. In such an environment of abundance, our country could afford to have the various sectors, public, private, not-for-profit, compete for a larger piece of the economic pie. Not coincidentally, our schools were the envy of the world.

Today, emerging economies throughout the world are effectively competing with the United States. Brazil, Russia, India, and China, often referred to as the BRIC countries, are winning the balance of payments war with the United States. Their economies are growing at historic rates, while ours at home is mired in recession and historically high, sustained rates of unemployment. And with this shift in the balance of economic power, the American standard of living is eroding. Not surprisingly, our schools have slipped from being top-rated to middle-of-the-pack mediocrity, behind places such as Finland and Singapore.

When I was growing up in the 1950s and 1960s, high school graduation was a significant factor leading to upward social mobility, but even those who failed to graduate could still be assured of a decent standard of living. High school dropouts could get factory jobs, put in 40 hours on the line, and earn enough to own their own home, have a car in the driveway, and send a kid or two to college. That standard of living started to erode with the oil embargo of the early 1970s when the price of gas began a steep upward climb from an average of about 30 cents a gallon to today's average of nearly $4 per gallon price. That's an increase of over 1,300%. This was the start of a massive outflow of funds from an oil-dependent country such as the United States to oil-producing nations such as Saudi Arabia.

During the Reagan Administration in the 1980s, the U.S. tax code was revised to reduce the tax burden for the wealthiest Americans. Supply side economists like Arthur Laffer, David Stockman, and Milton Friedman successfully argued that the wealthy would reinvest their newfound windfall in production, resulting in more and better paying jobs. The benefits were expected to "trickle down" to those less fortunate in the middle and lower classes. The effect, however, was markedly different from this expectation, resulting in the biggest redistribution of wealth in this country since the Great Depression.

For decades, the American middle class has attempted to retain the standard of living we were accustomed to by entering wives into the workforce in much greater numbers at first, and then later, through borrowing. When credit tightened dramatically after large investment companies collapsed in 2008, the bubble sustaining the middle class burst as well. Many jobs disappeared at the same time that home equity declined dramatically and even vanished overnight.

For the first time in history, more young people would rather go back to the past than into the future. Many Americans believe that their children and grandchildren will not be as well off as they were, and they're probably right. There are fewer and fewer well-paid positions requiring high levels of education and technical expertise, with much of the meager job growth that we've experienced since the collapse in 2008 taking place in low-paid service sector employment.

> If we're to reestablish hope and promise for those who depend on our schools for their share of success in the workplace, the public sector will need to work together more effectively with the private and not-for-profit sectors.

In such an environment, education is more important than ever before. However, the public sector alone has not been up to the task. High school graduation rates in the largest American cities struggle to reach 50% and have been stagnant for many years.[1] If we're to reestablish hope and promise for those who

depend on our schools for their share of success in the work-
place, the public sector will need to work together more effectively with the private and not-for-profit sectors. In fact, we will
need to eliminate the firewalls that have separated parts of our
society in the past and blur the distinctions that have prevailed
through much of the 20th century if we're to meet this important challenge.

During the last 10 years at the DOE, we relied heavily on
support from both the private and not-for-profit sectors. Major
new initiatives were invariably jump-started and financed with
private funds. Foundations like Gates, Carnegie, Soros, and
Bloomberg himself were responsible for such seminal work as:

- The New City Leadership Academy, which continues to
  train dozens of new principals annually for the reform
  work ahead;
- New small schools, of which more than 500 have been
  created in the last decade, and which represent the
  single most important breakthrough strategy, resulting
  in citywide high school graduation rates that have
  increased by 30% during that time;
- The Autonomy Zone, which later became known as
  Empowerment Schools, representing the first significant
  alternative to how large urban school districts can be
  managed in a decentralized manner.

These are simply three of many leading edge efforts which would
not have been possible without support from the private sector.

Similarly, the DOE received invaluable support from leading
not-for-profit educational providers like the Center for Educational Innovation, New Visions for Public Schools, Urban Assembly,
Institute for Student Achievement, the Internationals Network
for Public Schools, City University of New York, Fordham University, and many, many others in such areas as:

- New small schools design and implementation,
- School and network management services, and
- School transformation support.

Were it not for these pioneering contributors, those important achievements would not have been possible. In fact, the
New York City DOE required
that each new small school develop a partnership with an organization or institution in the
community as a prerequisite
for receiving the go-ahead to
create the school.

> The New York City DOE required that each new small school develop a partnership with an organization or institution in the community as a prerequisite for receiving the go-ahead to create the school.

Charter schools also rep-
resent a cross-sectoral effort.
During the Klein Administra-
tion, New York City became the most charter-friendly city in
America. For a time, the City itself was an authorizer, creating
more than 100 charter schools,[2] each of which had its own board
of directors who did not report to the DOE. Charters were given
shared space in DOE school buildings, and the DOE was instrumental in ensuring funding parity for charter schools.

In 2010, I was invited to serve on a panel considering school
reform issues at Teachers College, Columbia University (TC).
Little did I know at the time that I would soon retire from the
DOE and go to work at TC as a professor of educational leadership. I shared the panel with two faculty members from the
college, as well as a deputy secretary from the United States Department of Education.

Congressman Charles Rangel, representing the 13th congressional district, in which TC is located, co-sponsored the event,
which attracted a couple of hundred participants, including
Robert Jackson, Chair of the City Council Education Commit-
tee. Jackson had been lead plaintiff for a lawsuit brought by the
Campaign for Fiscal Equity, which resulted in a landmark decision that New York State needed to fund New York City schools
more equitably.

The event proceeded without a hitch but devoid of any new
ideas. Rangel appeared inattentive until he asked, "Why doesn't
the private sector just give our public schools more money?" My
colleagues on the panel wasted no time chiming in their support
for the idea that the private sector should contribute more to
public education. My response was that the private sector will

contribute to educational reform, but that we can expect it to do so on its own terms, by competing with public schools. Further, public educators should welcome such competition because it would invariably lead to new approaches and strategies that we could all benefit from. Jackson jumped up, pointed a long finger of accusation at me and said, "You go back to the Central Office and fix those broken schools instead of closing them!"

The private sector will invest in school reform to make money. If they can improve student achievement at a lower cost, they will be successful and invest more. It's what they do best and where they can contribute most if invited by government to compete with the public sector. The resulting school choice will invariably spur differentiation, competition, and innovation to benefit students and their families by resulting in new models of successful schools that could be more widely replicated by all sectors of society. Without this kind of private sector involvement, America could not have developed the technology to end World War II or put a man on the moon. Improving our schools is no less daunting a task, nor less important for the continued economic growth of our nation.

Having deregulated the airline industry and telephone company, it is only a matter of time before the K–12 education "business" is decentralized as well. Had we been more successful than we have been, perhaps this could have been postponed longer. However, the poor condition and performance of too many schools in urban communities throughout the country, coupled with the shrinking job market for those who fail to graduate from high school, makes it inevitable and imperative that we dismantle the bureaucratic monopoly that we have come to know as our public schools.

As with any deregulated industry, there will be failures. Remember PanAm and MCI? But there are currently public school failures resulting in abysmal student performance that we have done little about for years, and sometimes decades. It's the successes, however, of leading charter school operators like KIPP, Achievement First, and Uncommon Schools that have provided educational opportunity for students in some of our poorest urban communities. The original KIPP middle school in the Bronx is the best middle school in that borough. The Bronx Charter

School for the Arts is one of the best elementary schools in that community. Even though all have not succeeded, charter schools have proven to be good options for many students and families in places where there were no good school options for generations of families. These opportunities will only increase as the private sector continues to enter the field.

To be sure, there will be failures, as well as unethical school operators that will have to be exposed and eliminated, but there will also be remarkable successes, as there have been with charters, that we can all learn from. Fear that some may fail or even exploit, is insufficient reason to perpetuate a centuries-old public education monopoly that has not been up to the task of educating all of our children, at least through high school graduation with opportunities for further postsecondary study.

## CHAPTER 9

# Reform the Central Office

The most egregious error made by superintendents and school reformers is the attempt to reform schools without simultaneously reforming the Central Office. School districts are largely dysfunctional organizations that are all organized into functional department silos. More to the point, those who work at Central have a vested interest in keeping things as they are, with authority vested in them rather than with principals or schools. After all, these are the very people whose success in the old system had them promoted to positions in the Central Office in the first place.

Throughout my career as a teacher, and later as a principal, the Central Office was a remote, but powerful organization that hindered rather than supported the work I was engaged in to serve my students. The standing joke was, "Hello, I'm from Central. I'm here to help." Nothing could have been further from the truth. The Central Office didn't know the names of the children in my classrooms, had not met their families, nor understood the neighborhoods and communities these youngsters came from each morning and went home to each evening. Nevertheless, Central was empowered to determine what and how I and 70,000 other teachers, along with 1,700 other principals, would teach and how we would assess our students, and regularly exercised that authority in ways that most often defeated our best efforts.

Schools regularly paid more than they needed to by being forced to purchase through Central rather than simply go to Staples or other suppliers. The Central Office regularly passed on federal and state mandates, and not only didn't attempt to make these more manageable for schools, but rather, added immeasurably to the burden and distraction with new rules, forms, and reports of their own. Historically, Central would also pass on requests from politicians unedited, tying up time and resources, and making schools vulnerable to patronage and corruption. We were constantly distracted by the program or initiative of the moment, and these changed more frequently than chancellors, who came and went every 2 or 3 years. During my 39 years with the New York City public schools, I worked for 14 chancellors. Joel Klein had the longest tenure, serving for 9 years; and, Cathie Black the shortest, with only 3 months of service.

As already discussed, one major reform strategy in New York City during the Klein Administration was to close large failed schools and open more than 500 new small ones, including more than 100 charter schools. Many of the principals selected to lead were trained by our own Leadership Academy to reinvent school for themselves and their students. However, we placed these fledgling new schools under the same central and regional managers, who neither understood nor supported this reform initiative. They gave the new school principals every reason to do things the way they had been done in the schools we closed.

To remedy this, the NYC DOE created an Office of New Schools and placed it directly under the chancellor's supervision. Essentially, the role of this office was to protect these start-ups from the rest of Central. We also created an Autonomy Zone to further protect our strategic investment from Central and field operations intent on ensuring its failure in order to protect the status quo.

The lesson for reform-minded superintendents is that the Central Office is a big part of the problem rather than the solution. That realization, however, does not ensure that the district leader will easily find a way to neutralize the negative effects of Central on schools, let alone identify an alternative to how the Central Office has traditionally been organized and continues to function.

Recall Michael Bloomberg's response during his first run for

> The lesson for reform-minded superintendents is that the Central Office is a big part of the problem rather than the solution.

mayor of City of New York, first mentioned in Chapter 1, when he was asked why he thought his private sector managerial experience would transfer to the public sector. His response was that the jobs of public sector leader and private sector leader were essentially the same; that is, to recruit, support, incent, protect, and ultimately hold accountable the best managers that can be found. I firmly believe that excellent description can effectively be applied to school district leadership as well.

If we were to follow Bloomberg's example, the role of the Central Office would be limited to finding and recruiting the best principals available, and holding them and their school communities accountable for the highest levels of student achievement. If those were the only responsibilities of the District Office, Central would be reduced to a small staff supporting the superintendent, including legal representation, data and accountability, press and public relations, and human resources.

This district leadership model is based on the idea that Central is least effective when it attempts to directly influence what teachers do in classrooms, and most effective when it understands and is comfortable in the role of rewarding success and exacting consequences for failure. The Central Office needs to get these incentives right by providing support, resources, and additional remuneration for successful schools, while closing low-performing ones. Superintendents are in the best position to acknowledge when schools succeed, and when to intervene to give others a chance to do better in schools that fail.

As previously mentioned, earlier in my career I was deputy superintendent for high schools in the Bronx. For those unfamiliar with this borough, it is the only part of New York City on mainland United States, and only one of a handful of places in the world preceded by the definite article: *the* Vatican, *the* Hague, and *the* Bronx. More to the point, it is the poorest, most educationally challenged, and some would say politically corrupt congressional district in the nation.

When I arrived at the Bronx Superintendent's Office, there was a staff of 120 serving 20 high schools. The previous year, two other Bronx high schools were removed from our jurisdiction for poor performance, and placed in state receivership. The office was typically organized into functional units:

instruction, guidance, special education, technology, human services, and operations.

When asked which schools they were responsible for, every staff member said all of them. But when asked what exactly each was accountable for, the question invariably resulted in silence and quizzical looks. Everyone was responsible for everything, but no one was accountable for anything.

My recollection is that the graduation rate in 50% of Bronx high schools at the time was barely 30%, but no one at the District Office felt any responsibility or accountability for that. With the superintendent's approval, we reorganized into cross-functional teams, with each responsible for delivering comprehensive services to just a few schools, and accountable for the outcomes of students in those schools. This experiment was short-lived, as just 2 years later, the office was abandoned in favor of larger regional organizations. However, the existence proof had been established, and it looked remarkably similar to the way our best new small high schools were organized, into interdisciplinary teams responsible and accountable for student outcomes.

A few years later, I went to work in the DOE's Central Office, known as Tweed, and remained until my retirement 8 years later as deputy chancellor. Tweed was named after a corrupt 19th-century New York politician who was responsible for constructing the building the Central Office is housed within. I spent most of my time and energy reorganizing field-level operations from an area-based structure into a network-based one. Today, New York City public schools are uniquely structured into 60 non-geographic, self-selected, self-governing networks of 25–30 schools each.

One of my great disappointments during my tenure at the Central Office was my failure to convince the chancellor and his leadership team that we should replicate what happened in the Bronx High School superintendency, and replace siloed functional areas operating in isolation with little-to-no accountability, to a system of cross-functional teams responsible and accountable for high levels of student achievement in a manageable number of schools. I had numerous opportunities to float this idea, but was always unsuccessful in convincing Joel Klein and my colleagues on his staff to move in this direction. Despite my inability to restructure Tweed, I remain convinced that the resulting organization would have better supported schools to achieve higher student performance levels.

Those who believe that schools need to change, but that Central doesn't have to, don't understand the extent to which the District Office can prevent schools from evolving into more successful institutions. Central often attempts to dictate classroom practice, but always fails to do so because when teachers close the doors to their classrooms each morning they do whatever they feel is necessary for their students to succeed. However, the superintendent and Central Office are well-positioned to recruit and hire effective school leaders, reward them when they succeed, and exact consequences if they don't. To do so requires a lean, focused team, as opposed to the bloated bureaucracies that attempt to micromanage schools. Reforming the Central Office in this way is a pre- or co-requisite to real school reform that results in high levels of student achievement.

## CHAPTER 10

# Be Bold!

Sir Michael Barber is the Chief Education Advisor to Pearson Learning. Prior to this, he served as an education reform advisor to former British Prime Minister Tony Blair. Joel Klein hired Barber as a consultant to the DOE, advising Klein and his cabinet leadership team on matters of school reform. At the conclusion of one session with Barber, Klein asked him what he and Blair could have done better in their efforts to reform public education in Great Britain. Barber's response was, "We weren't bold enough."

Incremental change is the enemy of reform. It is not a strategy to successfully restructure a failed organization. Rather, it is a strategy to perpetuate a low-performing organization.

Failed organizations never reinvent themselves. Those within and responsible for the failure in the first place have developed rules, roles, and relationships over a period of years, sometimes decades, that invariably prove impervious to change. In education, however, we are accustomed to providing the principal and teachers in low-performing schools with vast sums of resources meant to do the impossible; namely, to be something other than what they are, and do things differently than they have always done. The result most often is nothing more than continued failure.

Beginning in the 1980s the Board of Education was referred to as an "intractable bureaucracy," which should be dismantled and completely rebuilt. Under Klein, we developed a different approach that proved successful. We built new structures outside the DOE as an alternative to one part of it, nurtured and protected the new structure, slowly shifted resources over time from the old structure we wished to replace to the new structure, and then phased out the old structure. This approach proved wildly successful.

The first example is how we phased out large failed schools. Rather than simply close a school and disperse students and staff, we stopped sending students to the school, but permitted it to phase out over a period of a few years. This created the opportunity to replace the phase-out school with new small schools in the same school building that were phased in carefully, one grade at a time, over a similar period of years. At the conclusion of this multiyear process, the large failed school was gone, and in its place was a campus comprised entirely of several new small and more successful schools.

A second example of the use of this strategy was the Autonomy Zone, created to give principals and school communities more autonomy and authority in return for greater accountability for student progress. Beginning with 29 schools, the Autonomy Zone, later known as Empowerment Schools, slowly developed over a period of years, and served to replace regional level organizations serving all 1,400 schools, with autonomous school networks. Today, the DOE is the only large urban district in the country organized in this way.

There are three aphorisms that are frequently used in education circles that reflect the resistance to change in our schools at any cost. They are:

1. If it ain't broke, don't fix it.
2. Don't throw the baby out with the bathwater.
3. Don't reinvent the wheel.

Let's examine each one.

**If it ain't broke, don't fix it** is often heard in the most dysfunctional schools. Despite the fact that these schools are as destructive to the faculty as they are to the kids, teachers are so fearful of change that they fight tenaciously to perpetuate them. Public hearings to review the fate of such institutions are often packed with staff members who maintain that closing their failed school would be a great disservice. This is repeated time after time even though the record would suggest that failed schools rarely, if ever, improve from within.

**Don't throw the baby out with the bath water** is another rallying phrase employed not infrequently in the most toxic school environments. If there is a part of these institutions worth salvaging, it's the staff, some of whom voluntarily choose to join new school planning teams. Some of our best new small schools in New York City were created by former staff members of schools that have closed. Even the worst schools have some dedicated and effective teachers who have figured out how to be self-motivated over the course of their careers. These teachers and supervisors deserve to continue their service, but not in the same school building. You never want to be in a position to open a new school in which some members of the faculty feel more entitled because they previously worked in the same building. The last thing a new school needs is ghosts from a failed school.

> Some of our best new small schools in New York City were created by former staff members of schools that have closed.

**Don't reinvent the wheel** is the most misguided aphorism of all. If we knew how to create schools where all of the students could be successful, we would have. The only way we're going to get there is if educators commit to more than reinventing the wheel. We need them to reinvent school for themselves and their students so that more students, if not all, can succeed to their highest potential. This represents such a radical departure from the schools we currently have that nothing short of a complete reinvention will achieve what is required.

One major reason why reformers are rarely bold and audacious enough to accomplish what previously seemed impossible is the fear of offending others. Don't worry about what others think who don't share your sense of impatience, if not downright outrage. It is you who should be offended, not they. What is more offensive than that poor children of color are not given equal education opportunity nearly 60 years after *Brown v. Topeka Board of Education*, that landmark Supreme Court

decision that forever struck down the foolish notion that separate could ever be equal?

Joel Klein was so fond of Theodore Roosevelt's "Man in the
Arena" quote that he carried a copy in his wallet that read,

> It is not the critic who counts; not the man who points out
> how the strong man stumbles, or where the doer of deeds
> could have done them better. The credit belongs to the man
> who is actually in the arena, whose face is marred by dust
> and sweat and blood; who strives valiantly; who errs, who
> comes short again and again, because there is no effort with-
> out error and shortcoming; but who does actually strive to
> do the deeds; who knows great enthusiasms, the great devo-
> tions; who spends himself in a worthy cause; who at the best
> knows in the end the triumph of high achievement, and who
> at the worst, if he fails, at least fails while daring greatly, so
> that his place shall never be with those cold and timid souls
> who neither know victory nor defeat.[1]

Over my desk at Tweed, I had a quote by Max Planck, the
German theoretical physicist in the late 19th and early 20th cen-
turies who won the Nobel Prize for originating quantum theory.
He is credited with having said,

> A new scientific truth does not triumph by convincing its
> opponents and making them see the light, but rather because
> its opponents eventually die, and a new generation grows up
> that is familiar with it.[2]

Both Planck and Roosevelt articulated the same truth; that
is, we will never change the world for ourselves and our children
if we fear to do so because of the critics and opponents who re-
sist the changes we need to achieve success for all, but especially
for those who need us to be bold if they are to have a chance
to overcome poverty and racial injustice through education.
In New York City today, as in urban areas through the United
States, you can walk into a Kindergarten class on the first day
of school and predict with frightening accuracy which students
will graduate from high school some 13 years later simply on

the basis of race and how well or poorly the youngster is dressed. Our job is to be bold enough to do whatever is necessary to defy these odds.

# Afterword

This book was written as a call to action to improve our schools. I wrote it for teachers, principals, superintendents, school board members, parents, policymakers, community activists, educational advocates, students of educational leadership, and everyone else interested in the future of our children. There is no prescribed sequence to my chapters, nor one that leads to a more effective reform agenda than others.

Where to begin? Act in the best interests of our students. Reject precedent and tradition as sufficient reason for inevitability. Be bold enough to make a lasting difference.

The most important lesson I learned is that each of us, wherever we fit into the "system," has the opportunity to make profound changes that improve the lives of those who study and work in our schools. My book will have fulfilled its goal if it becomes a well-worn, dog-eared handbook that readers and reformers refer to from time to time for ideas and inspiration.

# Notes

## Introduction

1.  New York City Department of Education. (2007). Graduation dropout reports, Cohorts of 2001–2007. Available at www.schools.nyc.gov/Accountability/data/GraduationDropoutReports/default.htm

## Chapter 1

1.  New York City Department of Education. (2012). 2011–2012 Progress Report results for high schools. Available at www.schools.nyc.gov/Accountability/tools/report/defaulty.htm=FindPR

## Chapter 2

1.  B. C. Ganus, H. S. Bloom, J. J. Kemple, R. Tepper Jacob, et al. (2009). *Reading First impact study.* Huntington, NY: Nova Science Publishers.
2.  T. Kolderie. (1990, December). Mike Strembitsky and site management in Edmonton. Available at www.educationevolving.org/pdf/Strembritsky-Site-Management-In-Edmonton.pdf

## Chapter 3

1.  For more information, see R. Alexander, with C. Doddington, J. Gray, L. Hargreaves, & R. Kershner (Eds.). (2009).

*The Cambridge primary review research surveys.* London: Routledge; R. Alexander et al. (2009). *Children, their world, their education: Final report and recommendations of the Cambridge Primary Review.* London: Routledge.

2. New York State, Office of the Governor. (2012, February 16). Governor Cuomo announces agreement on evaluation guidelines that will make New York State a national leader on teacher accountability. Available at www.governor.ny.gov/press/02162012teacherevaluations

## Chapter 4

1. New York City Department of Education. (2011, July 27). Mayor Bloomberg and schools chancellor Walcott announce results of new policy on teacher tenure. Available at www.schools.nyc.gov/Offices/mediarelations/NewsandSpeeches/2011-2012/tenureresults072711.htm

2. R. G. Fryer, Jr. (2011). Financial incentives and student achievement: Evidence from randomized trials. *The Quarterly Journal of Economics, 126* (4), 1755–1798.

3. A. Baker. (2013, January 7). City names 17 schools slated to close. *The New York Times.* Available at http://cityroomblogs.nytimes.com/2013/01/07/city-names-17-schools-slated-to-close/

## Chapter 5

1. A. Baker. (2013, March 1). Born as a tribute but faltering, a Bronx school nears its end. *The New York Times* (late edition), pp. A1, A18.

2. New York City Department of Education. (2012, June 11). Mayor Bloomberg and chancellor Wolcott announce that record number of students graduated from high school in 2011. Available at www. schools.nyc.gov/Offices/mediarelations/NewsandSpeeches/2011-2012/Grad_Rates_20120611.htm

3. New York City Department of Education. (2007). Graduation dropout reports, Cohorts of 2001–2007. Available at www.schools.nyc.gov/Accountability/data/GraduationDropoutReports/default.htm

## Chapter 6

1. W. Ouchi. (2009). The secret of TSL: The revolutionary discovery that raises school performance. New York: Simon & Schuster.

## Chapter 8

1. L. Layton. (2013, January 22). National public high school graduation rate at a four decade high. *The Washington Post.* Available at www.washingtonpost.com/2013-01-22/local/36472838-1-graduation-rate-dropout-rate-asian-students
2. New York City Department of Education. (2013). New district and charter schools. Available at www.schools.nyc.gov/community/newschools/default.htm

## Chapter 10

1. T. Roosevelt. (1910, April 23). Citizenship in a republic (speech delivered at the Sorbonne in Paris, France). Available at www.Theodore-roosevelt.com/sorbonnespeech.html
2. M. Planck. (1949). *Scientific autobiography and other papers* (F. Gaynor, Trans.). New York: Philosophical Library, p. 33.

# Index

# About the Author

Eric Nadelstern is a professor of practice in educational leadership and director of the Principals Academy at Teachers College, Columbia University. Prior to accepting this position he was the Deputy Chancellor for the Division of School Support and Instruction for the New York City Department of Education from 2009–2011, overseeing instructional and operational support to the city's 1,700 schools.

He has also served New York City public schools as Chief Schools Officer for the Division of School Support; Chief Executive Officer for Empowerment Schools, a citywide district reform initiative serving 500 schools that accepted performance contracting in return for major decision-making authority; Supervising Superintendent for the Autonomy Zone; Chief Academic Officer for New Schools; Senior Instructional Superintendent for School Improvement and Restructuring; Deputy Regional Superintendent for Region 2 in the East Bronx; and Deputy Superintendent for New and Small Bronx High Schools. As the founding principal of the International High School at LaGuardia Community College he created an innovative public secondary school for English Language Learners that has been widely replicated throughout the city and around the country.

During his tenure with New York City schools, Eric Nadelstern served in institute leadership roles at New Visions for Public Schools; Stanford University; Teachers College, Columbia University; and Bank Street College of Education. He has been recognized for his contributions in the classroom by New York City schools and awarded the Angelo Patri School Award for School-Based Management, the Anti-Defamation League and the International Partnership Award. He has authored and been the subject of numerous articles and interviews on his recent work creating a critical mass of new small schools to increase student performance, establishing school-based autonomy as a school district reform strategy to foster greater accountability for student achievement results, and reforming Central Office operations in the largest school district in the nation.

Printed and bound by CPI Group (UK) Ltd, Croydon, CR0 4YY

10/06/2025

14686699-0001